# Push Through to Victory

## BY: JOY A CRUDUP

**Title**: Push Through To Victory

**Author**: Joy A Crudup

**Copyright ©2026 by Author Name**

All rights reserved.

**Published by Pine Tree Press**

**PINE TREE**
P R E S S

www.pinetreepress.com

Printed in USA

# DEDICATION

*I would like to dedicate this journal to everyone who has experienced some hard times in their life and was able to Push Through. To those who are currently in the midst of a hard time, I hope this journal encourages you to Push Through.*

*Push Through to Victory*

*Klaim Every Victory Now*

# INTRODUCTION

Grace and Peace!

Thank you for the purchase and your willingness to embark on your new life journey. Thank you for allowing me, via this journal, to help you to "PUSH THROUGH TO VICTORY."

My "PUSH THROUGH TO VICTORY" journey began back in December of 2019. I had just had surgery due to a torn meniscus in my right knee. Immediately (2 days) after my surgery, I was to report to Physical Therapy, 3 days later.

I reported to Physical Therapy, and that's where "PUSHED THROUGH TO VICTORY" came to life… Three days a week I was in this facility working my knee via squats, lunges, and the elliptical machine. One day, while talking to my therapist, I made the statement, "I have to keep pushing through to victory."

During physical therapy, through the pain, whether it was raining or snowing, or just outright freezing, I showed up and did the work. This is the same mindset you have to have—that you will show up and do the work that needs to be done for you to become the best version of you!!

I started creating posts on Facebook with encouraging quotes and ending them with the phrase;

**"#PUSHTHROUGHTOVICTORY."**

This journal consists of a few of those quotes as prompts to get you on the journey to victory!!!

> **"A FALL ISN'T FINAL UNLESS YOU STAY ON THE GROUND."**

Since I can remember, falling (failing) has been viewed as something negative—something you never wanted to do because of the stigma of embarrassment that came with it. As I have grown and experienced life, I have come to understand the importance of failing/falling. YES! I said the importance of failing/falling. It is in these moments that we gain the opportunity to re-group and reflect on what occurred that caused the fail/fall.

Our failing/falling moments are our growing moments.

**Reflect on a time that you failed/fell. What did that look like for you? How did you PUSH THROUGH?**

_____

_____

_____

_____

_____

_____

_____

_____

_____

_____

_____

_____

_____

_____

_____

_____

_____

_____

_____

_____

_____

_____

_____

> # DON'T COMPARE YOUR LIFE TO OTHERS. THERE IS NO COMPARISON BETWEEN THE SUN AND THE MOON. THEY SHINE WHEN IT IS THEIR TIME.

If we believe that there is a higher power and that higher power is the creator of you and your entire being, then we ought to believe that the creator created us as the best version of ourselves that we could be. Therefore, comparing yourself to someone else is a slap in the face of your creator.

We should be grateful and appreciate who the creator created us to be and believe that who the creator created us to be is enough for us to be. We cannot shine brightly if we concern ourselves with the light of others. We dim our lights when we concern ourselves with the light of others. Doing so prolongs us from our shining time and, at the same time, prolongs their time to shine.

**Can you recall a moment when you thought someone's light was shining brighter than yours? How did you push yourself through in that situation?**

_____

_____

_____

_____

_____

_____

_____

_____

_____

_____

_____

_____

_____

_____

_____

_____

_____

_____

_____

> # Be selective with your battles. Sometimes peace is better than being right.

Everything does not deserve our energy; every battle is not ours to fight. It's not always about being wrong but doing what makes your heart feel right. Do not allow people or circumstances to dictate your actions and/or responses. Just because a person or situation is vibrating on a lower level, you do not have to join them. Maintain your peace at all costs!

**Think about a time when you had to allow your wanting to be right to take a back seat to your peace of mind... What was your thought process as you pushed through that moment?**

_____

_____

_____

_____

_____

_____

_____

_____

_____

_____

_____

_____

_____

_____

_____

_____

_____

_____

_____

_____

> # Inner Peace begins the moment you choose not to allow another person or event to control your emotions.

I nner peace is a choice. We can make the choice to have inner peace or, by not making the choice, allow others to make the choice for us, therefore giving them total control of our actions. Choosing inner peace allows you to be around people that upset you and made you cry with their actions and/or words, which have spread rumors about you and even stole from you, with your head held high, unfazed and unbothered. They expect you to continue to react to their pettiness, but inner peace says, not today! I oversee how I feel, act, and/or respond...

**Think about a time when your inner peace was at risk; what did you do to push through to keep it intact?**

_____

_____

_____

_____

_____

_____

_____

_____

_____

_____

_____

_____

_____

_____

_____

_____

_____

_____

> # It doesn't get easier. You just get stronger.

**I**f life were perfect there would be no hard times, there would be no struggle, everything would be easy. News Flash!! Life is not perfect; truth be told, perfect does not exist. When life seems to be life'n and you are in a dark space, this dark space is where you are being strengthened. It seems hard with no light at the end of the tunnel, yet you are making it through, you are still breathing, you are living, you survived it day by day, minute by minute. Because you made it through this dark time, you must know you can make it through the next dark moment—yes, there will be another and another dark moment. With each dark moment you get stronger and stronger in preparation for the next dark moment as well as for the next moment full of sunshine; both moments need your energy... Be grateful for the strengthening!

**Think of a time when you felt you were in a dark place with no light at the end of the tunnel. How did you push through? What strength did you gain because of that dark time?**

_____

_____

_____

_____

_____

_____

_____

_____

_____

_____

_____

_____

_____

_____

_____

_____

_____

_____

_____

> # First say to yourself what you would be; and then do what you have to do.

S ometimes we find ourselves stuck and in a dark space due to fear, doubt, and lack of belief in ourselves. It is during times such as this that we start to speak the "what we are nots" to ourselves. We say things such as "I can't do this or that;" "I'm not qualified." The Bible, in 1 Samuel 30:6–8, tells us how David was scared for his because the people wanted to stone him; David did what we have to begin to do—he encouraged himself in God. Let me tell you what that looks like: You're in a dark place and you don't see the light; instead of pondering on the "What if's" and the "what you are not's," remind yourself like David did in Psalm 139:14: "I am fearfully and wonderfully made." That is encouragement enough to help you push through and do whatever it is you need/want to do.

**Think of a time when you had to encourage yourself; what words of encouragement did you use? How did you feel after you pushed through and completed the task?**

_____

_____

_____

_____

_____

_____

_____

_____

_____

_____

_____

_____

_____

_____

_____

_____

_____

_____

_____

> ## At the end of the day, I'm at peace, because my intentions are good and my heart is pure.

There are a lot of people out here that do good deeds. They may do it because the organization they belong to has called for them to do it; they may do it because it is the latest fad, like the ice challenge a few years back. Some may do the good deed just for a photo opportunity, which looks good, but the person could really care less. Not only when you are doing a good deed, but whatever it is you do, make sure your intentions are pure and not for show. My mom used to say, "You can fool some of the people some of the time, but you can't fool all the people all the time!" You cannot fool God! Make sure the things you do are sincerely from the heart, not for people to praise you but for you to serve God.

Can you think of a time when you wanted to do something and your intentions for doing it were pure, but perhaps some of the people helping you had ulterior motives? How did you push through and keep your integrity?

_____

_____

_____

_____

_____

_____

_____

_____

_____

_____

_____

_____

_____

_____

_____

_____

_____

> "Every morning we are born again. What we do today is what matters most."

Every morning, I thank God for the wake-up call; some mornings I linger in the fact that everything after the wake-up call is a plus; therefore, every day I am living in the surplus of God's Grace and Mercy. In the Bible in Matthew 6:34, Jesus is recorded telling the disciples, "Take therefore no thought for the morrow (tomorrow): for the morrow shall take thought for the things itself." In today's society this is like the practice of mindfulness—being in the moment. Focus on the affairs of today; remember we must get through today to enjoy tomorrow. It is just like playing a video game; you cannot advance to level 2 until you complete level 1.

Think of a time when you felt anxious about what was supposed to happen the next day, but you knew the outcome for the next day was contingent upon what you did the day before. Write about how you pushed through to complete the task amidst your anxiousness.

_____

_____

_____

_____

_____

_____

_____

_____

_____

_____

_____

_____

_____

_____

_____

_____

_____

_____

> "Failure is an important part of your growth and developing resilience. **Don't be afraid to fail.**"
>
> *Michelle Obama*

As children we are taught clichés like "failure is not an option," "practice makes perfect!" Such thoughts have created individuals who do not respond well to failure; for them failure is the end. That does not have to be the case; failure can be exactly what you needed to force you to turn and go in the right direction. When you fail, look at it as if you failed forward to your next level.

**Think of a time in your life when you failed at something and, as a result, you did something different, which turned out to be much better for you than the thing you failed... Did it change your view of the failure? What were some of your thoughts? Did you grow from it, and what ways did you grow?**

_____

_____

_____

_____

_____

_____

_____

_____

_____

_____

_____

_____

_____

_____

_____

_____

_____

> # I am clearing space for a new chapter, filled with amazing opportunities, abundance, and magnificent *blessings.*

A midst the storms, failures, struggles, and setbacks, you made it!!! So, despite everything you may think you are not, the fact that you made it through shows that you are: Resilient; Determined; You are an Overcomer; You exude Perseverance; You are Committed; and You're Capable of Pushing Through! The next chapter is your Victory!!!!

As you **Push Through To Your Victory**, take this time to think about what you want your next chapter to look like—what are some of your goals and expectations, who do you want to be there with you, and what role will they play? What are you expecting from yourself in this next chapter?

_____

_____

_____

_____

_____

_____

_____

_____

_____

_____

_____

_____

_____

_____

_____

_____

_____

_____

# NOTES

_____

_____

_____

_____

_____

_____

_____

_____

_____

_____

_____

_____

_____

_____

_____

_____

_____

_____

_____

_____

_____

_____

_____

Push Through To Victory

29

Thank you for your support and allowing me to help you
PUSH THROUGH TO VICTORY!!!!

Send your feedback, suggestions, and stories of VICTORY to
pushthroughtovictory@gmail.com

# AUTHOR BIOGRAPHY

Joy A. Crudup is the founder of Push Through To Victory Inc. She is active in the community, serving on the Penrose Advisory Council and overseeing the Junior Advisory Council and the Community Advisory Board at Life Do Grow Farm.

Joy holds a Master's and a Bachelor's degree in Social Work. She was previously employed with the City of Philadelphia for 11 years, working at Health Center 6, the Department of Prisons, and the Philadelphia Juvenile Justice Service Center. Joy was a recipient of the 2021 Penrose Martin Luther King award and the 2021 Street Legends Community award for the community work she has done.

As a resident of the community, Joy has seen how the disparities in education, health, and community funding have adversely affected the black community. Working at the PJJSC, Joy has witnessed firsthand how flawed the Juvenile Justice System in Pennsylvania is, why the rate of recidivism is so high for our young black youth in the system, which ultimately leads to the same high rate of recidivism in prison. Joy can attest to the rise in crime, while education is declining. She has seen her neighborhood go from having two trash days to one trash day, yet the number of people in the community has increased due to investors buying family homes and renting them out by room to students.

Joy believes that the needs and the voices of the community ought to be heard by the politicians in Harrisburg and City Hall so that together they can implement policies that will make a difference for our future. As the late, great Shirley Chisholm said, "You don't make progress by standing on the sideline complaining. You make progress by implementation."

Currently, Joy is serving her community as a grief counselor for EMIR (Every Murder Is Real) Healing Center.

www.ingramcontent.com/pod-product-compliance
Lightning Source LLC
LaVergne TN
LVHW052039080426
835513LV00018B/2396